Miss Haverly & Miss Cavendish

MICHAEL CONGDON

WITH ILLUSTRATIONS BY
MARIE GAGNON

Copyright © 2020 Michael R. Congdon

All rights reserved. No part of this book may be reproduced or used in any manner without the prior written permission of the copyright owner, except for the use of brief quotations in a book review.

To request permissions, contact the publisher at

michael@om.nivorous.com

ISBN Paperback: 978-1-7357536-2-1

First paperback edition December 2020

This is a work of fiction. Names, characters, businesses, places, events, locales, and incidents are either the products of the author's imagination or used in a fictitious manner. Any resemblance to actual persons, living or dead, or actual events is purely coincidental.

For

Tuxedo

Critter

Tibet, Leonard, Prudence

Hudson, Ariel

Phobos, Deimos

&

The Bradenton House

At 2:50 p.m. the house lays in stillness.

At 2:55 p.m. the house looms with foreboding.

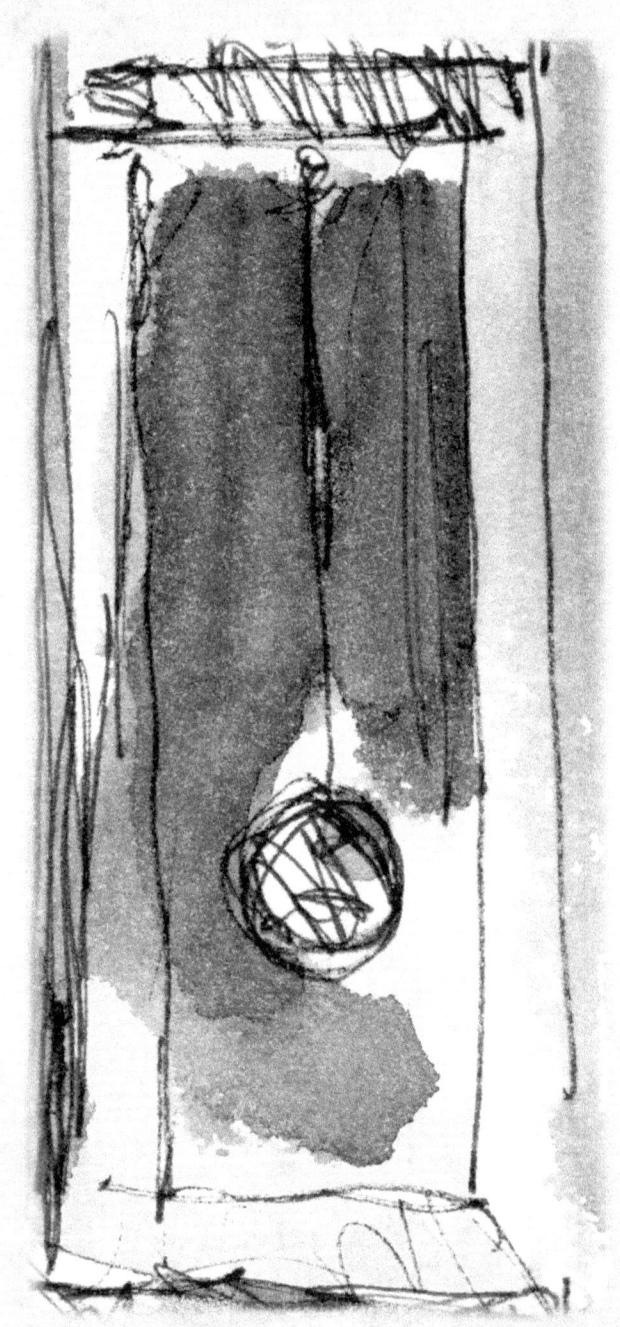

Inside, at 2:59 p.m. the only sound is the faint echo of a clock's ticking. As repetitive as a heartbeat, the once soothing sound saturates the cavernous conservatory in cacophony. Behind the warped wooden veneer and tarnished brass plates its rusty hammers groan laboriously as they lock themselves into a position to strike.

At 3:00 p.m. a deafening click breaks the hazy hush.

As hammers lurch and strike untuned strings, a slow, monotonous dirge vomits forth from the clock's belly. At length, a lone hammer taps the clock's pendulous brass chimes. Heralded by this violent outburst, a small, vintage, 1950's blown-glass ball falls from a browned and atrophied branch of a once-dignified Christmas tree long since fossilized. It rolls slowly across treacherously slanted floorboards coming to rest, at last, against a growing mound of other such spherical refugees. Over time these fallen decorations have erected a small dusty cairn in memory of their past glory, as they now rest atop a bed of crumbling brown pine-needles.

As the reverberations gradually fade, the conservatory is, once again, filled with a domineeringly silent and lifeless void.

At 3:01 p.m., rattling and scuffling can be heard from beyond a ground floor door.

Echoing through the emptiness, the once dulcet, now raspy and frog like voice of croaks, "Miss Haverly! Miss Haverly!"

"What?" is hoarsely bellowed from behind another one of the myriad doors on the second floor of the house.

From behind a distant swinging door on the ground level, "Miss Haverly! It's 3:01. It is past time for tea!"

"Again, Miss Cavendish?"

"I said, *Miss Haverly! It's 3:01. It is past time for tea!*"

"Indeed, Miss Cavendish, so I have been told."

Neither emerges from behind her respective door, thereby adding to their habitual rancor, and thus these wretches remain in a continual stalemate, as neither will be the first to rattle her chains in despair. This unseen scene's absurd repetition is something that neither Miss Haverly nor Miss Cavendish will admit to – let alone its tragicomic potential.During a couple hands of canasta many years ago, Miss Haverly and Miss Cavendish discussed the concept of humor and laughter. After a few minutes of like-minded discourse, they concurred that humor, which is forced, is not humorous at all – merely a juvenile attempt at recognition.

Following this, Miss Haverly and Miss Cavendish decided to focus on their own laughter. On that sultry September night, the neighborhood was the unwitting witness to the most horrific, maniacal howls bellowing forth from the opened windows of their antebellum home. Henceforth, the neighborhood agreed to avoid Miss Haverly and Miss Cavendish. Back in the conservatory, Miss Haverly and Miss Cavendish concluded that laughter was akin to a monkey's screeching; therefore, the act of laughing was unseemly and did not have any place within their home.

Although laughter is verboten, Miss Haverly and Miss Cavendish do entertain the idea of guileless humor. Even they occasionally allow themselves a vague amusement by the innate, and often accidental, strength of nature versus mankind's inherent ineptitude and general stupidity.

The neighbors suspect Miss Haverly and Miss Cavendish are merely entertaining themselves in the twilight of their lives – however disagreeable it or they may be. Two Junes ago, after their morning's repast, Miss Haverly and Miss Cavendish were on the veranda puffing on their cigarettes when they espied a glistening spider's web constructed just past the verandah's paling. The pristine web's anchors were fastened to the decaying stone steps' rusted banister and to an august magnolia tree that abutted the front porch. Morning dew clung to its viscid, taut strands. At the web's heart, a yellow, brown and blue striped spider bided its time. It was esurient, inconspicuous, substantial and poisonous. After debating this natural wonder, Miss Haverly and Miss Cavendish wandered back inside to dress for tea and summarily, the arachnid was considered irrelevant.

During tea, Miss Haverly and Miss Cavendish were in the conservatory playing canasta. The routine creak of their mail slot opening, the letters shuffling to the floor, and the squeaky tap of the mail slot closing were duly ignored. However, seconds later, while Miss Cavendish was laying down her 120-point meld, they heard a scream from just on the other side of their front door. Being marginally curious, yet thoroughly exasperated, both sighed as they simultaneously stood up and shuffled to the large bay windows. From behind the thick, dark drapes, they discreetly observed the postman as he shrieked and danced while flailing his arms around him. Eventually, he grew ghastly pale and collapsed, lifeless, on the flagstone path. Silence resumed, the drapes were closed, and odious grins were smeared across the once vexed faces of Miss Haverly and Miss Cavendish as they returned to their game of canasta.

A few years later, the same magnolia tree which had housed the spider, was infected with a rot that was slowly killing it. Thus a branch that was quite large and quite dead constantly creaked and cracked about fifteen feet in the air. Honestly, it should have been removed long ago, but Miss Haverly and Miss Cavendish saw no need as it wasn't doing anything dangerous.

During another fateful afternoon a newer postman was delivering the mail. After dropping it off through the front door's mail slot he descended down the front steps. It was this point that the creaking of the branch became a loud snap, broke off the trunk and fell to the ground with a thud and crunch.

The neighborhood has a new postman now.

At 3:02 p.m., Miss Cavendish dodders about behind a café-style swinging door. Delicate clinking is briefly interrupted by a cat's hiss and growl. The next few seconds of silence are abruptly shattered with a squawk, "Take that, you miserable imp!"

Miss Cavendish's retort is immediately followed by the muted thud of something hitting the wall. Hissing, caterwauling, and the scratching of feline claws against wood ensues, and in short, the delicate clinking starts again.

Slowly, a large, bustled posterior emerges as it pushes open the door. What remains of the fabric is entirely black. Simultaneously, a geriatric cat rushes from beneath Miss Cavendish's ankle length skirt, escaping the confines of the kitchen. Wild-eyed, it darts as quick as a 14-year-old cat can with the fear of being stepped on or kicked again.

Prudence has lived with Miss Haverly and Miss Cavendish since they found her as a kitten hiding in the musty crawlspace where house met earth. Their lack of interest and her curiosity for food and shelter kept her in their company. Although they named her Prudence, Miss Haverly and Miss Cavendish often refer to her as "it", "imp", or "fleabag". Fleabag is, perhaps, the most appropriate name since she is infested with hundreds of parasites. Reckless upheavals randomly commence as she suddenly attacks her scabrous black and nicotine-stained yellow fur with furious scratching and biting. Even while riddled with mange, she continues her quest to seek and destroy the fleas, ticks and mites that consume her. Prudence is a bit high-strung and unaffectionate, as neither Miss Haverly nor Miss Cavendish interact with her. The only time she appears comfortable around humans is between 3 and 4 p.m. daily. Ironic that this routine starts with a quick kick to her ribs and being dashed against the kitchen wall.

Presently, she is in her usual spot on the mantelpiece. Languidly curled around a large, overflowing columbarium, she licks and chews on a stale cigarette stub she deftly pawed out from the ashes. On the hearth directly below her, a small pile of pierced butts and shredded stubs spreads. While Miss Haverly and Miss Cavendish take their tea, she will spend the hour feeding her fix, preening her patches, or attacking any flea that has moved in the way of her jagged, dulled, and nicotine-stained teeth.

3:03 p.m., Miss Cavendish continues hobbling toward the baroque tea table while clenching a Pall Mall between her garish red lips. With each throaty, rattling inhalation her cigarette smolders. Clouds and whisper-thin trails of smoke hover in the thick air behind her with nowhere to go and no way to dissipate. With both hands at her waist, she bears an overwrought silver tea tray and matching service. Proffered with these tarnished relics sits two florid Royal Doulton teacups with matching saucers, sugar bowl and creamer, in their lives' ochre twilight, as well as what was once a dainty plate which presented a few currant scones, and two small glass bowls holding raspberry preserves and clotted cream.

Miss Cavendish's short-lived cigarette's cremains pepper the entire tea service as she feebly makes her way across the conservatory, engulfing the room with an acrid fetor of stale, dried sweat, tobacco smoke, and attar of rose. Her forward gait is accompanied by a visage of acute pain that reflects her scorn over her role as tea server; one which she claimed many years ago. With each step, her trussed fishbone-white and corpulent thighs tap the edge of the tea tray. A quiet but repetitive rattle forewarns her arrival, like the quiet and subtle rumble one hears before an approaching train. Miss Cavendish careens forward with a momentum fueled by ire, pride, and nicotine, while clouds of smoke lazily trail behind. Nothing will stop Miss Cavendish from reaching her destination. (That the dilapidated china will survive its arduous journey to the table is merely a side benefit.) With a final thud, Miss Cavendish drops the tea service on the small table, the metallic rattling ceases.

After a silent pause, a voice croaks through the empty room. Miss Haverly pauses before her descent down the stairwell, looks at Miss Cavendish and venomously spits. "Miss Cavendish! I will take my tea black and hot."

A cigarette is clutched firmly between the knotted knuckles of her arthritic hand. Twitching with palsy, this hand animates Miss Haverly's atrophied arm with the semblance of life. As she descends the staircase, her back against the wall she brushes herself against many large, dusty, desiccated paintings. Over the years, this daily movement has left a smeared yet clean slash along the wall and the hanged portraits as her bodice repeatedly attracts the minute bits of dust, paint and tar which forms a murky film over every surface in their house. While still holding onto the railing, Miss Haverly wildly puffs away on the cigarette, which somehow re-appeared, from her deathlike grip to between her thin, creviced lips.

As Miss Cavendish begins pouring she flatly retorts, "Of course you will my dear Miss Haverly."

A steamy, pungent aroma of bergamot wafts over her as the boiling concoction violently gushes from the teapot's spout and splashes into, on, and around the chipped and stained cups. As the thinly cracked saucers' shallow bowls fill with the potent broth from the overflow, the rims appear, from above, like narrow atolls surrounded by and filled with the same dark and heavy-scented sea. Ashes from the dead cigarette, still clenched between Miss Cavendish's lips, drift down and briefly float, eventually drowning in their murky grave.

Miss Haverly and Miss Cavendish have never taken cream or sugar in their afternoon tea; thus, the proffered cream and sugar remains unmolested, as it always has. Such rituals like this, like biting one's fingernails, tend to be engrained. For them it is a mere formality. The decorative sugar and cream hurts no one, except the sugar and the cream themselves as they look just as delectable as Miss Haverly and Miss Cavendish.

As Miss Haverly reaches the landing, her shaky, undead hand appears on the banister's newel. Gently and slowly caressing the rounded knob, a lengthy, cold ash from her cigarette drifts to the floor, landing on a pile of previous newel-massaging, ash-dropping afternoons. With both women standing in the same room, the reek of urine, tobacco, camphor, and lavender emanating from Miss Haverly and the noisome stench of stale sweat, tobacco, bergamot and sickly-sweet rose swirling around Miss Cavendish, the conservatory chokes and gasps for life from their miasmal decrepitude.

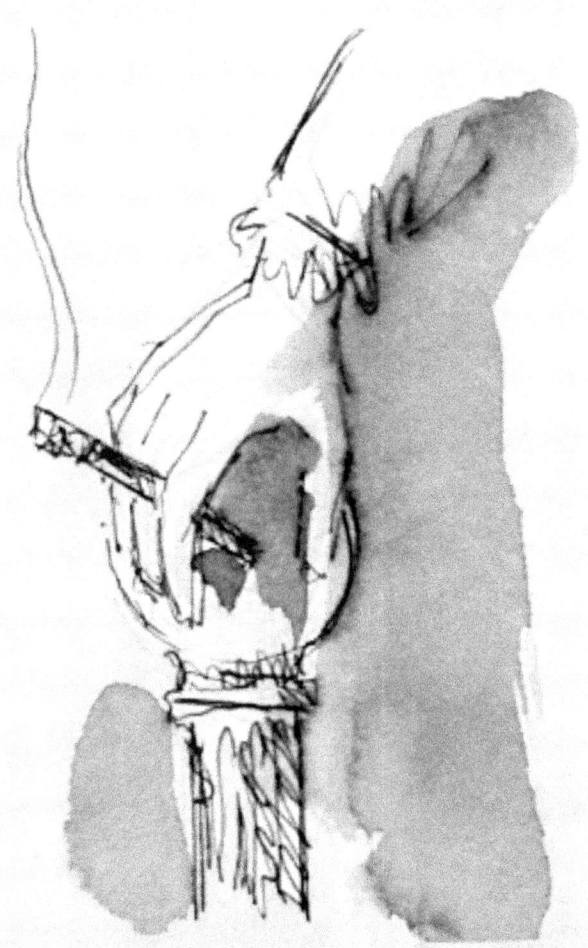

Prudence blinks, unfazed, then continues to lick and chew on a cigarette butt.

At 3:05 p.m., the conservatory is cloaked in silence as Miss Haverly and Miss Cavendish take their seats. Silently, they sit face to face and finish their Pall Malls while they wait for the tea to cool to a tolerable temperature. The fraught languor is heavy – thick like copious layers of cerements upon an ancient corpse.

Prudence paws another filthy stub from the ashes.

At 3:08 p.m., Miss Haverly, a withered old crone, is seated at her favorite chair; a Spanish ladder-back an ex-husband brought from Spain decades ago. This cruel, Catholic legacy of the Spanish Inquisition is a sadistic back-straightening device that she has grown fond of. Miss Haverly believes good posture indicates proper rearing. Thus, even though the chair was originally created for torture, it now has a well-worn air of masochistic comfort as the original walnut stain has faded from where her lumbar region, waspish hips and posterior naturally rest against its railed back and wooden seat. From a distance it has a rustic and inviting look, yet sitting in it feels unnatural, and is quite painful. Not even Prudence dares to nap on this chair and always gives it a wide berth whenever she takes to stalking the conservatory.

Miss Haverly's face is pallid from the lack of sun. Keeping to her skin's wan coloring, she applies an impenetrable layer of base and foundation to cover the deep crevasses and fissures that began as wrinkles years ago. Her deep-set eyes are lined with thick smudges of kohl. The natural weeping of her deteriorating tear ducts, her drooping eyelids, and the constant dabbing of a kerchief forces the black rings to widen as her sclera become bloodshot from constant abrasion. As Miss Haverly wears no other make up, her visage transforms daily: morning – an ancient, syphilitic whore, afternoon – a hydrophobic raccoon, and evening – psychotic termagant.

Miss Cavendish takes her tea whilst seated on a tattered chesterfield. Its once plush blue and green pinstripe velvet has matted down and faded. Small round burn holes, and a filthy film of dust, cigarette ash and cat fur have ruined the fabric. The only questionably clean spot is the cushion where Miss Cavendish always sits. However, after years of resting her ample weight in the same spot, the padding in the cushion has broken down leaving a permanent dent in its thick batting. The width of the chesterfield is too narrow for Miss Cavendish's buttocks, so she is accustomed to leaning forward with her knees drawn together and her lower legs akimbo. With the arms and back of the chesterfield equal in height and Miss Cavendish always hunching forward on the same decaying cushion, she appears as a child with progeria sitting on an oversized couch. Occasionally, Prudence can be found curled up in a ball, napping on one of the other cushions, but Miss Cavendish believes this behavior is obnoxious and unacceptable. A common animal on the furniture is not respectable.

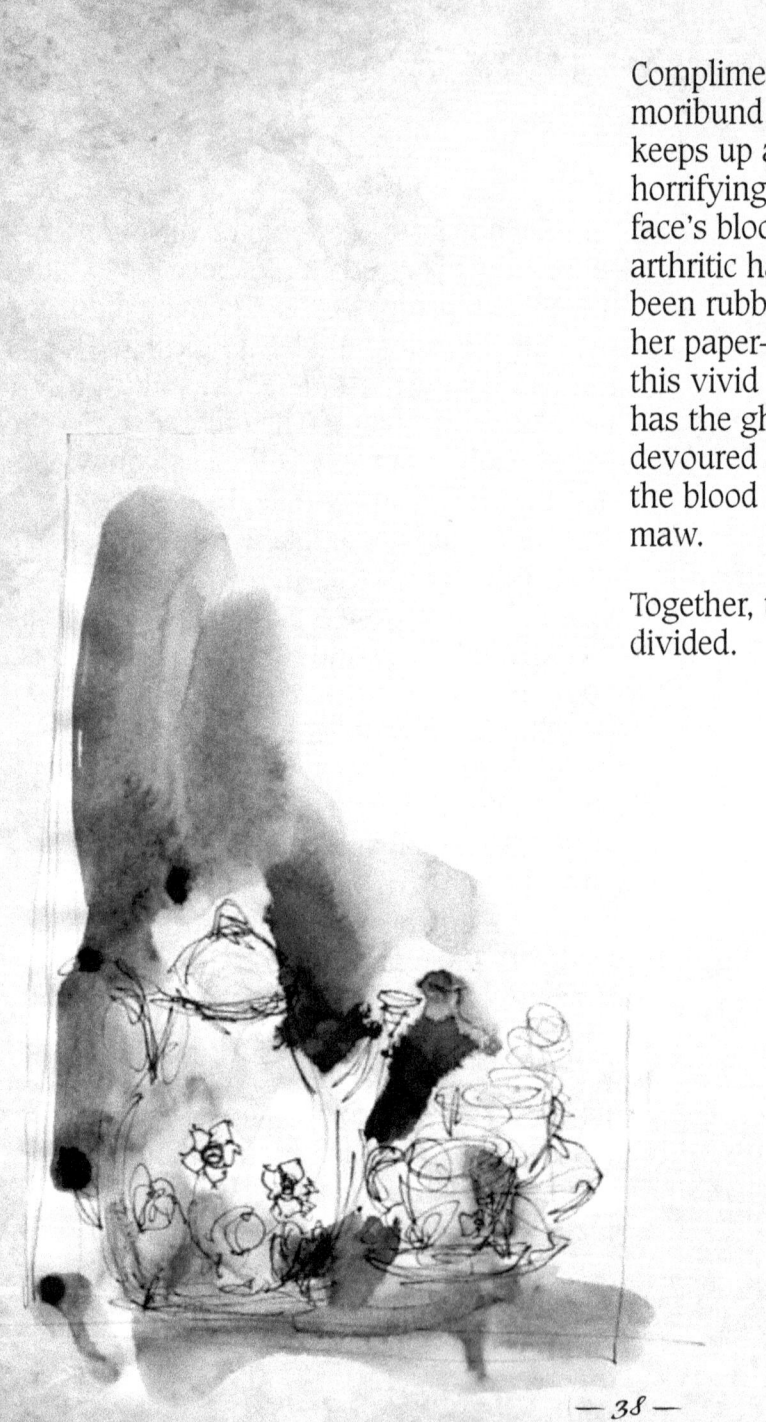

Complimenting Miss Haverly's pallor and moribund grotesqueness, Miss Cavendish keeps up appearances by focusing on her horrifyingly rufescent lips while ignoring her face's bloodless skin tone. With shaky and arthritic hands, the vivid iron red, having been rubbed ferociously across and around her paper-thin lips, is always uneven. With this vivid and smeared gash Miss Cavendish has the ghoulish appearance of having devoured a fresh kill, and has yet to wipe the blood and bits of viscera away from her maw.

Together, they are a single ghastly face – divided.

Every morning Miss Haverly and Miss Cavendish assist each other with their corsets; lacing them tight to the point of strangulation. Their persistent attempts for the fitted hourglass shape have ceded to age and nature working against them; Miss Haverly's mien now is as a human-sized anorexic wasp, while Miss Cavendish's is as a corpulent, quivering, gelatinous lump. Each retires to her individual boudoir where she dons black grenadine mourning apparel á la late 1800s *de rigueur*. These remnants of once-austere dresses, like daguerreotypes, have rotted with age. Tears, small moth holes, stains, thinned fabric, lost buttons, cigarette burns, and frayed hems make their dresses fit for a banshee.

Neither is concerned about the degraded state of her wardrobe.

During the belle époque, Miss Haverly and Miss Cavendish were highly esteemed within the elite cliques of society; thus, they were taught to always keep up appearances. Although they accrued a small handful of ex-husbands, most had died, a few were divorced, and two were institutionalized for rather obscure psychoses, these two grand-dames have always remained ladies-in-waiting. As then, even now, Miss Haverly and Miss Cavendish never know when suitors might come a-courting.

Miss Haverly and Miss Cavendish are still seated in silence. The currant scones' decimated remains and the cooling tea is ignored. With so little to say, each scarcely acknowledges the other's presence. Like every day between 3 and 4:00 p.m., Miss Haverly and Miss Cavendish will pass the time gazing into the lacing and leatherwork of their tattered, Catherine boots, or when not scrutinizing their footwear, they broodingly study the antiquated portraits lining the walls of the conservatory and stairwell.

Erstwhile lifelike representations of their ancestors, the quantity of dilapidated remains portrays a decadent history of grandeur now lost with time. As housecleaning and upkeep is a low priority for Miss Haverly and Miss Cavendish, these once vibrant portraits, that represented the painters' skills during the Realism Movement the mid-19th century, have been reduced to washed-out faces floating in a sea of black painted canvas that swirls and eddies about them with dark and dusty shades of blues and reds. Neither remembers who these people were or where they came from, nor do they care. The paintings exist in their home and that is adequate. Why they stare and what they search for is unknown.

A closer inspection of the portraits reveals that the eyes are still quite vivid. Æons after creation, they continue to eerily follow people whether in the conservatory or on the stairwell. The artists' uncanny technique provokes gratuitous gossip amongst the busybodies in the neighborhood. Some believe that the unnatural stares of the dead imply an already crowded house to Miss Haverly and Miss Cavendish. Others guess that visitors rarely accept invitations owing to the eyes' intimidating preternatural stares that gaze upon the living like a tribunal or crazed mob. Whatever the opinion, apart from a paucity of suitors calling on them, neither Miss Haverly, nor Miss Cavendish care about receiving company.

For them, the point is moot.

At 3:10 p.m., Miss Haverly and Miss Cavendish are crushing their cigarette butts in a large carved crystal ashtray that overflows with the remains of innumerable Pall Malls. Suspecting that they are depositing new kitty treats, Prudence pauses from shredding her prey and scrutinizes their movements. A queer look from Prudence and she immediately begins scratching the scabs on her neck.

Miss Haverly's back is to a large bay window. Its heavy black curtains are open, suffering the conservatory with the diluted, foliage-dappled daylight through the exceedingly decayed, grimy and tar-stained Point-de-France drapery. Thus an uncanny ambience settles down upon the conservatory. As Miss Haverly adjusts herself, she acquires a rotting-yellow hue. Above their heads a wobbling and creaking ceiling fan slowly spins, forcing the stifling air and parlor's dank stench upon them. From two decadent yet dilapidated Tiffany lamps, copious cobwebs lazily sway and drift upward like sea kelp. None of this interest Miss Haverly or Miss Cavendish – it is of no importance.

Miss Haverly and Miss Cavendish lift the teacups to their lips. As they fussily sip at their tea, the slurping sound they produce is similar to a vampire's attempt to suck the last drop of blood from a corpse. After shakily returning the teacup to its flooded saucer, Miss Haverly removes a scone from the tray and begins to pick at it. She digs out an offending currant and deftly flicks it into the hearth.

A small *Tink* is audible as each stale, dried currant she recovers hits its mark with the deadly aim of an assassin's precision. ... *Tink* ... Meanwhile, Miss Cavendish snatches a small gilt cigarette case off the end table next to her chesterfield. ... *Tink* ... Another Pall Mall makes its way to her lips where she wets it with her grey, cracked and pasty tongue. ... *Tink* ... She secures her cigarette between her receding, paper-thin, and rouge painted lips and ... *Tink* ... grabs a dusty glass ball wrapped in tarnished, filigreed silver. ... *Tink* ... As she lights her cigarette and returns the filthy table lighter from whence it came, she reduces almost one-quarter of her cigarette to ash with one rattling, wheezing inhalation. ... *Tink* ... By this time, without eating it, Miss Haverly has thoroughly annihilated her scone. ... *Tink* ... All that remains is a pile of desiccated crumbs lightly covered with a smearing of clotted cream and a dollop of raspberry preserves that slowly bleeds down from atop her unappetizing mound of mush.

... Tink ...

At 3:15 p.m., Miss Haverly presses the threadbare, starched pleats down with her gnarled and bone-thin hands and leaves a slight trace of dampened handprints upon the rotted and wrecked grenadine. Miss Cavendish repeatedly smoothens and tucks the skirt of her dress around the sides of her waist and underneath her hips; giving her ruined and fleshy thighs a brief reprisal of their former supple glory. Subtle streaks of sweat are visible for mere moments before being absorbed into the moth-eaten and tobacco infused substance that once was a blend of silk and wool.

They begin adjusting their coiffures. Miss Haverly pushes at her receding hairline and scalp with the padding of her knobby fingers – searching for any wispy white hairs that secretly gained freedom from the prison of her painfully tight bun. With any discovery, her fingers twist the fine hairs together and cram them into the wadded mass of hair that awkwardly but firmly rests upon her head.

Miss Cavendish preens what little she has on her head using her index finger that is liberally coated with a sludge made up of crumbs and dry sputum. The thick amber locks of yore, which accorded her fame as a great beauty, are now gray, thinning patches of short hair that barely conceal the large brown and red spots of melanoma marbling her pate. Her constant attempts at rearranging are pointless. Moments after positioning her hair, it falls back, more pronounced, glistening and clotted with crumbs.

Prudence licks at the raw patches of her skin.

Their attempts fail; however, neither Miss Haverly, nor Miss Cavendish sees any reason to stop her habitual routine no matter how manic she may appear.

At 3:18 p.m., immediately after finishing their cups of tea, Miss Haverly fills both teacups to the brim with more bergamot tea. The saucers' scented seas flow over onto the silver tray, yet again.

Miss Cavendish sarcastically sneers, "Yes, I want more tea."

Miss Haverly heavily sets the teapot down and bluntly responds, "Now, we can't let the tea go to waste, can we Miss Cavendish?"

She holds out a silver bowl, "Sugar?"

Miss Cavendish snaps back, "No."

Miss Haverly purposefully drops the sugar bowl back onto the tray with a minor crash, "Nor I, I do believe."

Silently, Miss Haverly and Miss Cavendish reach for another scone. As Miss Haverly hunts and pecks for the scone's repulsive currants *Tink* and Miss Cavendish slathers an inappropriate amount of clotted cream onto hers, *Tink* they briefly pause and gaze toward the clock. Without looking, Miss Haverly flicks another currant at the hearth.

… *Tink* …

For a while, the ethereal butterfly curls of cigarette smoke, the ceiling fan's slowly rotating blades, the linked metal chain tapping against the chipped glass lamp that loosely dangles from the fan's center, and the whole mechanism subtly rocking back and forth, unbalanced, are the only movements in the otherwise silent conservatory.

The hands of the looming grandfather's clock show 3:21 p.m.

... *Tink* ...

At 3:21:02 p.m., Miss Haverly and Miss Cavendish stand up.

Miss Cavendish whispers, "Is it time?"

Miss Haverly responds in kind, "Yes."

Their suffocating air of dour, bitter matronhood transforming into mischievous auras of youth is unsettling. Almost gleeful and trembling, Miss Haverly and Miss Cavendish's voices hint at excitement and impatience.

Slumping forward, Miss Haverly stands stock-still in front of her Spanish chair while staring at Miss Cavendish and nervously announces, with a hand over her mouth as if she is about to blurt out a secret, "I'll go."

Trembling, Miss Cavendish replies, "Yes, I suppose it is your turn, isn't it Miss Haverly?"

While giving her approving response, Miss Cavendish loosens the lacing around her wrist cuff and pulls a damp and curled stamped envelope from her sleeve. Miss Haverly's withered arm suddenly appears within snatching distance of the letter and her gnarled fingers snaps at it like a vulture ripping apart a carcass. Her swift movement startles Miss Cavendish, thereby causing her trembling hands to drop the letter. Before she realizes it, Miss Haverly, is lurching

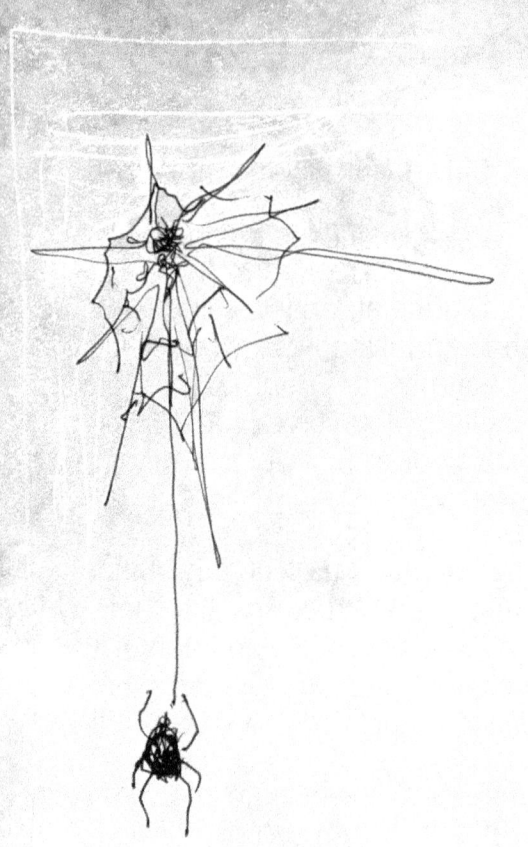

toward the front door with the crumpled letter flailing about at the end of her undead arm. Miss Cavendish leans over, grabs another cigarette from the gilt box, and lights it. With one long wheezing and heavy inhalation, she burns the Pall Mall half way down. While she watches Miss Haverly shamble toward the front door, Prudence watches her with her mouth cracked open and her nose flared as she inhales the toxic fumes Miss Cavendish expels from her raw and ulcerous throat.

As Miss Haverly approaches the front door, she reaches up, with her good arm, and drags a tattered mantilla down from one of the prongs jutting out of the wooden coat rack. She catches many of its moth-eaten holes with the prong and tears it; creating larger singular split. Once the mantilla is finally freed from the rack's fingers, she hurriedly drapes it over her head and around her shoulders. She grabs a dirt-stained, wicker gardening hat and firmly forces it on her head; tightly securing her torn scarf in place. Finishing this ensemble, she seizes the sunglasses that sit half buried under stacks of unopened mail, which precariously tower and lean on a small stand next to the door and roughly shoves them over the bridge of her nose and scarf. The flaps of her ears, well hidden by the mantilla, are pressed down from the hat and jut out into two little silken points from the sunglasses' earpieces pushing between them and her head.

While Miss Haverly busily enshrouds herself before leaving their crepuscular realm, Miss Cavendish shambles over to the tar-stained lace curtains, where she draws the drapes. A stifling darkness descends on the dank conservatory except where the sunlight bleeds through tiny slits of worn fabric in the decrepit drapery.

Miss Haverly opens the front door. As she makes her way through the threshold, she securely closes the door behind her with a slow creaking that abruptly ends with a thump. Slowly, she heads down the steps to a flag stone path that eventually leads to the street before her. As she finishes her descent, with her hand on the railing in a vice-like grip, Miss Haverly looks back at the house. Seeing the curtains drawn, she turns around and begins to plod over the stones and weeds, faintly nodding to herself.

Meanwhile, Miss Cavendish peers from the side of the curtains. She observes Miss Haverly's movements like a raptor watching its prey. In the close darkness, she quietly mutters to herself.

"If she picks a magnolia flower, then I wait at the staircase landing. If she does not, then I open the drapes and return to the chesterfield for the rest of our tea."

Miss Haverly reaches the shrubbery that blocks sight of their garden from the street. While hidden from the neighbors' prying eyes, Miss Haverly leans over, even further, and noisily sniffs at a vivid purple flower from one of the many monkshood plants which dot the border around their poison garden. As she rises, she quickly glances down the road. For a few minutes, Miss Haverly stands motionless, like a deer

listening for encroaching unfamiliar sounds. In a flash, her limp limb appears above her head. Its quivering fingers coarsely caress a blossom from the towering magnolia tree. As quick as it grasped the flower, her shriveled arm is at her side. The fleshy petals spin as she roughly twirls its stem. Finally, Miss Haverly drops the flower and heads toward their sagging veranda. As she reaches the steps and grasps onto the railing, she notices that the curtains are still drawn.

Three decades ago, the city required them to post a plaque in front of their antebellum home, as it is one of the few remaining pre-Civil War structures in town. Due to its age, the house occasionally attracts many bored and roaming snowbirds – much to the chagrin of Miss Haverly and Miss Cavendish. Every winter they have to ignore the doorbell or pretend they are not home. They do not like random people traipsing around their home while asking about its pointless history. For the last ten years Miss Haverly and Miss Cavendish have grudgingly accepted tourists in their home, but only on the 23rd of December between the hours of 9:00 a.m. and noon. At which time both Miss Haverly and Miss Cavendish go about their morning routine largely ignoring them, their questions and any insightful comments they may wish to share. Unfortunately, they were to either place the city's commemorative tablet on a pedestal in their yard, or be heavily fined. While monetary issues are beneath Miss Haverly and Miss Cavendish, bureaucratic red tape is worth even less notice.

When Miss Haverly and Miss Cavendish inherited and took up permanent residence, they came across the family deed to the house and surrounding land that dated back to 1739. Most of the previous residents had been born, lived, and died within these walls. Today, almost 300 years later, with little if any repairs, the house is the chalky outline that remains after the body has been taken away. Perhaps the flaking paint had been touched up. Perhaps the stone steps that lead to the front porch had once been restored. Perhaps someone replaced the antique fixtures and wired the house for electricity years ago. But nothing has been done for decades now and the house is in dire need of repair.

This house was built on 100 acres of private land. When times called for it, their ancestors would sell off parcels of the family's land. The natural grace and beauty of their property would be stripped away and houses for new families would be erected. These homes would stand sound for decades. Then more parcels of land would be sold off and another generation would arrive, tear down, and build up prefab houses bought from the Sears, Roebuck & Co. catalogue. Eventually, only the two acres of land on which the house stands would remain and an entire neighborhood filled with ranch-style homes improperly built, weak, inferior, and disposable little boxes, grew around them. The neighbors were just as disposable, just as weak and just as inferior – moving around like ants building up and tearing down to fit this faster paced era. Today, sturdy, well-built houses of the upper middle class with desires for grandeur have replaced earlier, ranch-style homes. While the neighbors began to take bits and pieces of history and incorporate them into their personal architectures, against the test of time, Miss Haverly and Miss Cavendish's ancestral home remains standing – mouldering in its own decrepitude.

The front façade consists of a narrow veranda that sits three feet above ground. Six steps, made more from mortar than stone, rest between two tall columns connecting the flagstone path to the front porch. Above the veranda is an enclosed balcony. Two lead-glass French doors opening onto it are separated by three large oriels projecting out onto the balcony. The domes' arching, but brittle and rotted ribs blend into the roof while their corbels' fragile remains taper to three individual balls that rest against the house's main wall on the veranda. Above this, where the angled roof meets the walls, a wood-planked widow's walk circumscribes the house. Two small attic alcoves jut from the slanted roof to the perimeter of the lower porch and balcony's main wall, each containing small octagonal windows. Another, larger oriel protrudes further from the attic close to the corner of the roof. Its cylindrical shape ends with a bulbous spire on which a weathervane rests. This pointed dome is covered with bird droppings and a large hole exposing the decaying structural beams. In the center of this alcove a French door opens to the walkway. On each side of this door is an octagonal stained-glass window. Their rosette patterns are grimy and ruined from neglect and generations of rain, dust, and muck. Two large marble gargoyles sit on the Doric columns framing the front center of the house. These 3 feet tall, eroding, marble rain spouts rest in front of the widow's walk at foot level. Rain gutters set on the roof just below the walk slant downward into the rear opening of the gargoyles.

Straddling the house are two enormous, soot-crusted, and cold brick-chimneys that slowly became aviaries for mockingbirds, finches and bats. The roof of the house severely sags in the center. However, it has a few good years left before it eventually succumbs to the relentless rains of a future hurricane, upon which its collapse will kill all who live within the walls while they sleep.

Two magnificent magnolia trees grow on the outer sides of both columns framing the main entrance. The rest of the house is surrounded and concealed by fifteen feet of

jungle-like copse made up of numerous oak, magnolia, cedar, eucalyptus, and coniferous trees, all of which are draped with Spanish moss. Their acreage is lined with a dense and thorny hedgerow, as is the base of the house. The amount of fecund flora imposing upon the moldering manor suggests nature is trying to reclaim its land as it pushes on all sides to defeat and devour the man-made structure. Apart from Miss Haverly and Miss Cavendish's neglected poison garden, which is "this" far away from going to pot, the remaining yard is overgrown with weeds and littered with countless fire ant hills.

The house resembles an overgrown mausoleum.

Before Miss Haverly ascends the steps to the veranda, she stops and sticks the crumpled letter into the mailbox. After turning up the American Pride mailbox flag, she looks back at the stone pathway and mutters,

"The weeds need pulling."

Slowly, with her white-knuckled grip grasping the railing that lines the steps, she ascends to the front porch. Miss Haverly gives a deep and rattling sigh, opens the front door, and reenters her private Stygian abode.

Structure, like this house, is cursed to endure.

At 3:25 p.m., having already donned her own mantilla, Miss Cavendish stands at the foot of the stairs waiting for Miss Haverly to return from the garden. Once inky black with vivid red roses woven into its silk, her shawl's red threads are faded and the black fabric is dulled and stained giving it a semblance of a stretched and shapeless ancient tatted black doily. The moth-eaten and shredded train extends down her back, almost dusting the ground with each wobbly step she takes. The rest of it drapes around her hunched shoulders. Miss Cavendish's deep-set eyes anxiously gaze at the door while her blood red lips clench down on another cigarette, its ashes softly falling upon her ruined shawl.

Miss Haverly turns from closing the door. Seeing Miss Cavendish wait eagerly at the foot of the stairs, she walks past her and begins to climb the steps. Curtly, she announces, "Let's go."

Miss Cavendish immediately falls behind Miss Haverly and nervously opines, "Yes, I think I will join you today."

Step by step they climb the stairs in unison. However, Miss Haverly and Miss Cavendish ignore the railing and bannister. Instead, they move like geriatric cats on the prowl. Sensing this, Prudence decides to join them in their festivities. After reaching the stairhead, Miss Haverly and Miss Cavendish's pace quickens. Not wanting to be left behind, Prudence darts ahead and waits at the door located at the far end of the hallway. Pacing back and forth, she rubs her flanks, cheeks, jowls and chin against the door's smooth finished surface, while Miss Haverly and Miss Cavendish hastily hobble toward the door.

Halfway down the hall, Miss Haverly produces a rusty key from a hidden hip pocket and keeps it jutted between her arthritic knuckles. It bounces with each unbalanced step, yet remains pointed toward the door. A faint sweat from her sudden exertion entices the key to slip, and her knuckles grow whiter from tightening their firm grasp.

As the two women reach the door at the end of the hall, Miss Haverly's trembling hand tries to fit the key in the slot. The marks of her repeated failed attempts are immediately lost in a sea of scratches nicks and dings that now texturize the brass plate and wood surrounding the keyhole. Not helping the situation, Prudence weaves herself between Miss Haverly's unsure legs. Eventually the key finds its mark and smoothly slides into the tiny, dark orifice. With a quick turn to the right and a faint click, the door cracks ajar. Miss Cavendish licks her lips, moistened with excitement, while she rocks

back and forth in place – ready to bolt from her position when given the opportunity.

Miss Haverly withdraws the key and heaves the frail shoulder of her lame arm against the door. Silently it swings open revealing a small landing and the bottom step of another set of stairs rising off into the darkness beyond. Prudence, wide-eyed, scampers up the stairs and vanishes from sight. Miss Cavendish, still rocking back and forth, looks at the chain which dangles from the ceiling of the stairwell and then sizes up Miss Haverly, "Miss Haverly, as you are a bit taller than me, will you please turn on the light?"

Miss Haverly turns her dangerously bowed body and lifts her face so she can stare up into Miss Cavendish's eyes. She sneers, "Again?"

Louder and with more anxiety, Miss Cavendish begins to whine and physically shake, "Miss Haverly, please turn on…"

Interrupting her, Miss Haverly snaps at Miss Cavendish, "I heard you the first time!"

Miss Haverly steps forward into the shadows and promptly her decrepit arm hangs from a frayed cord dangling from the fixture of a single light bulb above her head. As she lets the dead weight pull the cord

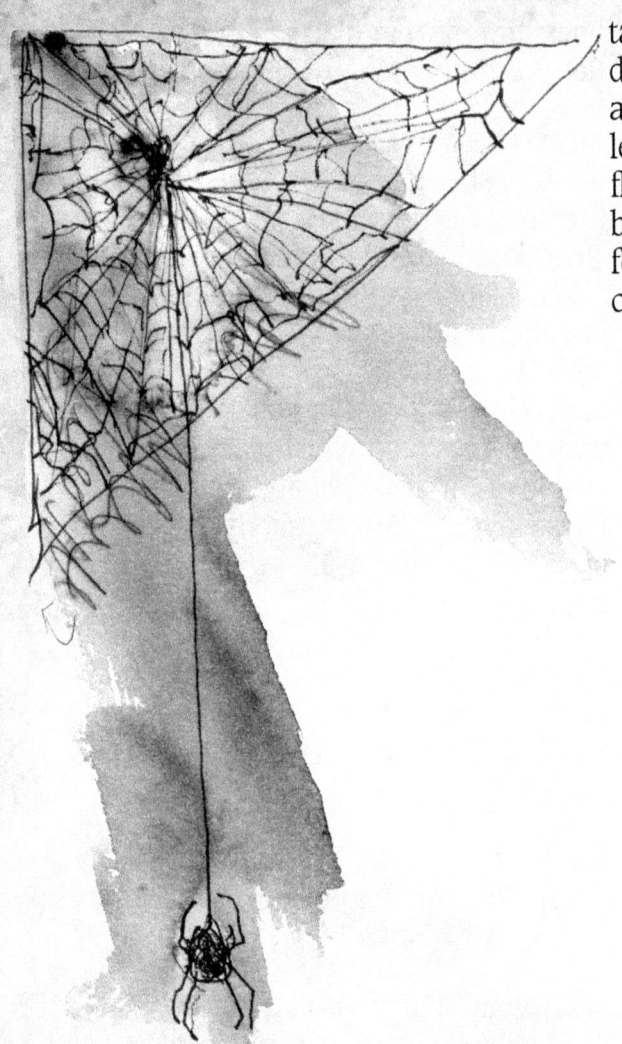

taut, a harsh white light cuts through the darkness and briefly blinds Miss Haverly and Miss Cavendish. Miss Haverly's fingers let go of the cord and her arm immediately flops down to her side while the cord snaps backward bouncing around in space for a few moments before it comes to rest in its original position.

Growing accustomed to the light, Miss Haverly and Miss Cavendish start climbing the full set of steep, narrow and well-worn wooden stairs. The veneer of every tread's middle is a worn away, exposing the original color of the cherry wood attesting the centuries of use. Along both walls of the stairwell underneath an ample layer of dust, the treads have retained their rich walnut-stained finish. The slanted ceiling is stained an uneven yellow from tar, age, rot, and water damage. The signs of deterioration drip like thinned paint onto the tongue-and-groove walls. Running up the center of the ceiling, is a thick grey electrical cord. The primary purpose is to carry electricity to the attic. The secondary purpose? A nesting ground for spider's eggs and subsequent attachment points for the woven tapestry of spider webs that heavily looms three feet above their heads. Hanging on the walls either side of the stairwell are numerous gilt-framed, oil-smudged ovals and rectangles of black.

Miss Haverly and Miss Cavendish passionately inhale their cigarettes – leaving a trail of stale smoke behind them as they climb toward the musty camphorated sea of stifling heat and harsh humidity.

At 3:30 p.m., Miss Haverly and Miss Cavendish are standing and wheezing at the top of the stairs; in part to the thick, musty and stale air and in part to the infernal heat, but truthfully in response to their emphysematous lungs. Both women drop the remains of their cigarettes on the floor next to their humidity-cracked leather Catherine boots.

Miss Cavendish's hand blindly searches along the wall next to the stairwell for another small chain. The attic's dreary gloom is erected from shadows lying atop shadows. Stacks of old furniture resting inside and protruding from the two side alcoves block the small windows. Shafts and drops of sunlight mottle the attic with its limited access. Between the two alcoves is a large cylindrical oriel. The filthy stained-glass rosette windows are made of cobalt, iron and copper glass pieces. Slices of light cut through the edges of the yellowed sheet-cum-drape, which hangs over the central door's window thus promoting the attic's eerie shadows with a disagreeable marbling of sunlight hither and thither.

Miss Haverly and Miss Cavendish stand at the threshold of their family's sepulcher, and its striated stench of musty camphor, rust, rot and decomposition is almost suffocating. The faint padding from tiny paws and the light clicking of feral claws belie small rodents hiding from the light and imminent danger. Without warning, aggressive scratching and shredding emanates from the gloom and penetrates the near-silence.

As Miss Cavendish's hand reaches the chain, she quickly pulls on it and a dim light appears over their heads. Try as it may, the incandescent light cannot cut through the abyssal shadows that permanently exist. Even though some of the thin layers are peeled back, the persistent deathly gloom remains. Miss Haverly and Miss Cavendish can see the concrete objects for what they are. Growing inward from the slanted, tongue-and-groove walls of this mouldering chamber are piles of wood crates, cardboard boxes, ancient and desiccated leather trunks, suitcases, hope-chests, chairs, rusted iron bed-frames, sagging, rotted mattresses with their batting falling out from rats having chewed away at their cotton covers, tables, old canopies, portrait frames of all sizes, broken chandeliers, piles upon piles of clothing, towering stacks of termite infested books, an old work bench with rusted craftsman tools and gardening implements, sewing machines, a rocking horse, and a loom. Hanging from hooks above the workbench dangled many types and sizes of saws, and a single scythe. In one corner a pair of shackles are bolted to the floor. Scattered across the entire attic are the tiny sinewy bones of thousands of small rodents. Meanwhile, the tearing and scratching continues.

Miss Haverly and Miss Cavendish wind their way along the narrow path that weaves through the looming junk of their ancestral ossuary. Reaching the three small steps that lead to the alcove's riser, they find Prudence already, aggressively shredding the sheet as she scratches through it at the door that lay beyond. Looking at each other with excitement in their eyes, Miss Haverly reaches over and deftly scoops up Prudence with her good arm and rests her in her wasted arm and roughly scratches the cat's chin.

Miss Cavendish places her pudgy liver-spotted hand on the knob. Her voice thick with phlegm, she looks back and asks, "Is it time, Miss Haverly?"

Still scratching and picking at Prudence's patchy and scab covered chin, Miss Haverly's eyes cut the thick air with disgust as she stares intently into the slits of the cat's half-open eyes, "Let's go."

Without further ado, Miss Cavendish turns the tarnished brass knob and small hidden latch unhooks. Swinging inward, the door presents the glorious sunshine upon her haggard face as the attic explodes with light. What was once cloaked in shadow, is now naked – tamed by the sun's radiant beams. In unison, both hiss.

At 3:35 p.m., Miss Haverly and Miss Cavendish step through the doorway and onto the widow's walk. At once, Miss Haverly turns and drops Prudence back into the attic. From this elevation, they can smell the sea's salty air on the wind that commenced moments earlier. Like banshees, they skillfully circumscribe their home with their dresses and mantillas flailing about.

Prudence trots from the attic out into the sunlight. Promptly and silently, she leaps up to the railing and precariously crouches, adroitly balancing herself, waiting for Miss Haverly and Miss Cavendish's return. Her eyes contain the thinnest razor-black line as she basks under the sun in the fresh air, like a sphinx.

While Miss Haverly and Miss Cavendish walk they do not speak. Only the sounds of their creaking footfalls on the walk's rotted wood, their brushing away the smaller tree branches that abut and have overtaken the pathway, the scraping of thicker branches against the whitewashed and rusty iron railing and the whistling wind as it whips through their wispy raiments' remnants hint at their present location. Although Miss Haverly and Miss Cavendish are obscured by many of the old trees that had grown higher than the widow's walk, occasionally, their gossamer forms appear like shadows drifting from bough to bough. Only the stately magnolia trees at the front of the house are tall and full enough to completely conceal them from prying eyes. As these two harridans reach the final corner, they pause. Having a perfect and protected view of the street and the neighbors' homes beyond the hedgerow, they bide their time.

At 3:40 p.m., a U.S. Postal Truck sits unoccupied as the driver makes his daily rounds. In this particular neighborhood the mailboxes are located near the front doors. Sharing in the gossip, helping spread a rumor, or discussing similar interests while delivering the mail, the postman is on a first name basis with most of the residents. More than mail delivery, he is a grapevine which keeps the community connected, or at least, informed about its various dalliances and scandals that every community wishes kept under the carpet. Ambivalent about the individuals, he uses the conversation to keep his job enjoyable and entertaining. This is sufficient.

Four houses away from Miss Haverly and Miss Cavendish, the postman is busying himself discussing some trivial matter with a neighbor. This neighborhood is a new route for him since he was assigned it a year ago, after an accident that, after dubious circumstances, left the prior postman a paraplegic. The new postman, a squat paunchy man with wan and mealy skin emerges from the front porch. He wears a regulation pith helmet, long white socks, black and highly polished shoes, navy blue shorts, and a light blue short-sleeved shirt. His satchel is slung over one shoulder. After shoving his free hand into it, tinny classical music coming from a hidden radio increases in volume and drifts on the wind. Shuffling through the stack of mail in his hand, he heads to the next house – oblivious to everything around him.

At 3:43 p.m., Miss Haverly and Miss Cavendish hide behind two tall eucalyptus trees that block the corner of the walkway. They look at each other and, with an unnatural grace slink toward the thick boughs of their magnolia trees. Again, Miss Haverly makes eye contact with Prudence who hisses at her as she passes. Continuing to the concealed safety of the magnolia trees a soft, distant thud is heard behind and below her. Inching further into the tangled mass of branches that block her and Miss Cavendish from wandering eyes, Miss Haverly turns back and sees that Prudence is no longer in view. As she looks out onto the yard, a cruel grin forms on her parched and paper-thin lips. From their aerie, Miss Haverly and Miss Cavendish watch the postman head toward their adjacent neighbor's front door. Miss Haverly leans further over the railing. Her vestigial arm thrusts out and, blindingly quick, its withered fingers pluck a magnolia blossom. She twirls the flower beneath her nose and makes a long, deep death rattle. Sweat begins to bead on her forehead as she drops the flower and looks down onto their yard, "The yard is overgrown. Weeds and moss everywhere."

Miss Cavendish nods as she gently caresses the gargoyle's smoothed marble skull. Her pudgy and knotted fingers occasionally flick away the dried bird droppings.

At 3:45 p.m., Miss Haverly and Miss Cavendish can overhear bits of the conversation from next door as it drifts upon the wind.

"That stupid old cow ... the head of the PTA." A female voice exclaims. She is in an uproar about something.

"Yeah? What did she do this time?" The hollowness of the postman's concern goes unnoticed by their neighbor.

"...bless her little heart, but I think she's a bit tetched ... position only because she's the daughter of Mayor ..." the neighbor's voice suggestively implies that she is worried.

"She's always seemed fine to me, at least whenever I ... but I have noticed ..." the postman acknowledges her concern with agreement.

"Exactly! Her children run wild and she ..." Their neighbor exclaims.

"I've always found her kids to be pleasant enough. You know whose kids need ..." The postman starts in with his share of gossip for the day.

"... thank the Lord someone else sees ... Now my children ... husband calls them his 'little angels'." The neighbor is excessively sanctimonious.

As their neighbor mentions her children, both Miss Haverly and Miss Cavendish spit at the ground. One morning last autumn, while sitting on their veranda, they caught these 'angels' trespassing onto their property to eat the small black berries they had decided were truly blackberries. Later that afternoon, during tea, the police and the children's mother interrupted Miss Haverly and Miss Cavendish. The children were terribly sick from belladonna poisoning and the shrubs that grew pressed up against the house were suggested to be the culprits. Miss Haverly and Miss Cavendish pointed out that had the little darlings not trespassed and eaten berries from a shrub that didn't belong to them, then none of this would have happened. The least the little darlings could have done was to ask Miss Haverly and Miss Cavendish if they could have some – they were, after all, sitting on the veranda at the time of the occurrence. Miss Haverly and Miss Cavendish were forced, by the city, to destroy the offending bushes from their front yard – and pay for their removal.

"… I'm sure as I can be about … At least that is what I have been hearing. But, you know …" The postman continues in a hushed tone, giving the impression that the information he gives her is not to be spread around.

Weaving between the vapid conversation and the wind rustling through the trees, Miss Haverly and Miss Cavendish can hear Mozart's *Eine kleine Nachtmusik*. Among the three sounds the ripe and sultry, salty wind is the most pleasant.

Eventually, the conversation leads to the weather and plans about a possible summer vacation for the children. The postman responds tersely. He has given and taken all that he needs before continuing up the street.

"Have a good afternoon!" Her squeaky voice calls out.

He smiles and waves to their neighbor as he emerges from her yard and into the street.

At 3:52 p.m., the postman walks toward Miss Haverly and Miss Cavendish's home. Presently, the hedgerow that gives their overgrown yard privacy from the street hides him while his footfalls and humming grow closer. Unbeknownst to the neighborhood, one of their gargoyles has a larger, more amorphous shadow than usual as Miss Haverly and Miss Cavendish have ducked between the magnolia tree and the stone beast.

The postman stops where the hedge separates and the flagstone path meets the sidewalk. Miss Haverly and Miss Cavendish espy his pasty and liver-spotted arms as he shuffles and organizes the mail. Surprised to find only one letter, an advertisement, he shrugs, turns, and heads up the overgrown path. His monotonous humming changes to tuneless whistling. With each note expelled, Miss Haverly and Miss Cavendish tense. As he begins to climb the steps that lead to their veranda, Miss Haverly and Miss Cavendish, look at each other. Their mouths crack open and they grotesquely, yet sincerely, smile.

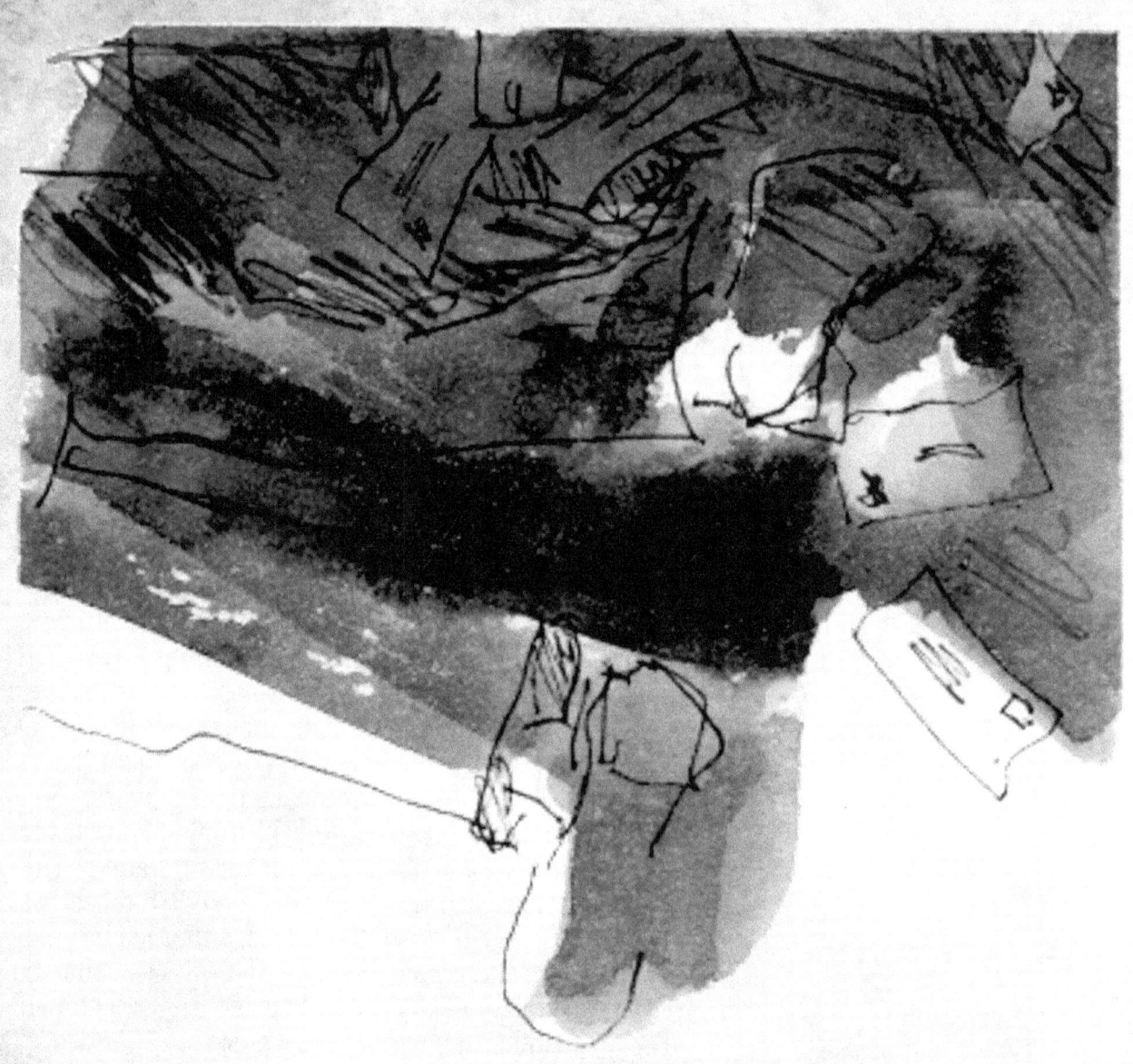

At 3:53 p.m., Miss Haverly and Miss Cavendish hear the mail slot's creaking hinge as the postman delivers their mail. Shortly, they hear the scrape of rusty metal against itself as the postman attempts to retrieve the letter in the mailbox. After a few failed attempts, the postman grunts and the hinged mailbox door squeakily succumbs to his will.

During his struggle with the mailbox, Miss Haverly and Miss Cavendish decide to see what the postman is up to. Their arthritic and edematous knees do not permit them to stand up unassisted; therefore simultaneously, they strongly grasp and lean against the gargoyle for support. As they stand upright, they hear a din of rustling leaves and small branches breaking. This is immediately followed with an, 'Aiiigh' which is promptly interrupted by a loud crunch and thud directly below them. Mozart continues to blare but the whistling has ceased.

Miss Haverly and Miss Cavendish lean over the railing just after the 200-year-old gargoyle tips off from its perch. Directly below them, the hapless postman lies under it – crushed, akimbo. They watch, motionless as his pith helmet rolls away on its brim. Letters and advertisements spill out from his overturned satchel. A flash of gold briefly blinds Miss Haverly and Miss Cavendish as his wedding band glistens in the sunlight. A thick branch laden with magnolia flowers rests across his head. His mouth is agape. He sputters, chokes and finally coughs up a small stream of blood from his open lips and gouged cheek. It trickles down his chin and onto the massive, exposed and gnarled roots of their magnolia just as the flitting violins introduce the Rondo: Allegro.

Like Miss Haverly and Miss Cavendish, he too is motionless.

At 3:58 p.m., Miss Haverly and Miss Cavendish, flick their cigarette butts over the railing, look up, and wince at the clear bright sky. Over the gulf, towering black thunderheads are quickly moving inland. In a matter of minutes a late-summer storm will overtake the neighborhood.

Miss Cavendish turns her gaze to Miss Haverly.

"Better now?"

Miss Haverly, quickly glances at her then returns to the black and brooding horizon. Her voice is caustic.

"Of course."

Miss Cavendish crosses the threshold of the opened attic door and Miss Haverly follows in step, closing the door behind them.

GLOSSARY

Akimbo	*turned outward*	Grenadine	*silk/wool mix*
Antebellum	*pre-Civil War*	Guileless	*without deception*
Arduous	*difficult*		
Atoll	*ring-shaped reef*	Hydrophobic	*rabid*
Atrophied	*wasted away*		
Attar	*essential oil of roses*	Mantilla	*lace/silk scarf*
August	*distinguished*	Maw	*mouth, muzzle*
		Miasmal	*foul-smelling*
Belle Époque	*settled and comfortable life prior WWI*	Mien	*specific look revealing mood*
		Miscreant	*scoundrel*
Camphorated	*saturated in camphor*	Moribund	*point of death*
Cerements	*sheet in which to wrap a corpse*	Mouldering	*slow decay from neglect*
Columbarium	*ash holder; urn*	Newel	*knob*
Copse	*group of trees*	Noisome	*offensive smell*
Corbel	*support beam*		
Corpulent	*fat*	Ocher	*yellow-brown*
		Odious	*revolting*
Daguerreotypes	*old photographs*	Ossuary	*bone room*
de Rigueur	*required by fashion(*		
Dour	*severe, stern*	Pallid	*bloodless, pale*
Dulcet	*sweet sounding*	Palsy	*involuntary tremors*
		Pate	*person's head*
Edema(tous)	*dropsy*	Paunchy	*protruding gut*
Esurient	*hungry, greedy*	Paucity	*insufficient quantities*
		Preternatural	*beyond natural*
Fecund	*fertile*	Progeria	*premature aging*
Fetor	*foul smell*		
Florid	*overelaborate*	Rancor	*long-standing bitterness*
		Rufescent	*red*
Gilt	*painted in gold leaf*		
Gossamer	*fine, delicate*	Saprogenic	*produced by decay*

Sanctimonious	*smug*
Scabrous	*indecent, salacious*
Sclera	*white of the eye*
Sepulcher	*burial place*
Striated	*stripe, streak*
Stygian	*dark, gloomy*
Termagant	*overbearing woman*
Truss	a *support, frame-work*
Verboten	*forbidden*
Vestigial	*functionless, residual*
Visage	*facial expression*

www.ingramcontent.com/pod-product-compliance
Lightning Source LLC
Chambersburg PA
CBHW081509080526
44589CB00017B/2699